FAST FOOD

EASTER

EXPLORING THE MEANING AND SIGNIFICANCE OF THE DEATH AND RESURRECTION OF JESUS

BY DARREN

Kevin Mayhew

First published in 2000 by
KEVIN MAYHEW LTD
Buxhall
Stowmarket
Suffolk IP14 3BW

0 1 2 3 4 5 6 7 8 9

ISBN 1 84003 485 8
Catalogue No 1500324

Cover by Darren
Edited and typeset by Elisabeth Bates
Printed in Great Britain

Contents

FAST FOOD SERIES

JOSEPH
DAVID
PETER
MOSES

THE STORY OF JOSEPH WITH CONNECTIONS!
THE STORY OF DAVID WITH CONNECTIONS!
THE STORY OF PETER WITH CONNECTIONS!
THE STORY OF MOSES WITH CONNECTIONS!

FAST FOOD CHRISTMAS

Look out for further titles

Introduction

This is the second of two books (the other being the Christmas story) that follow a similar format to the previous *Fast Food* books but with the teaching focused on an event rather than the life story of a character. That said, however, since both books cover the two events central to the Christian faith – the incarnation and the cross – all teaching evolves around the person and work of Jesus.

In coming to these powerful and complicated events, my aim was to communicate the foundational truth behind each as clearly as possible. The truth, detail and implications of both the incarnation and the cross can, I feel, often be overlooked within children's material, with a more simplistic approach chosen and the rest left for a bit later in life. Yet from my own experience, the older you get the more it is assumed you already know the foundational truths of such events and consequently you gradually drift into an awareness of them wondering why you hadn't realised it before!

I believe it can only be beneficial to a deeper understanding of the person and work of Christ to begin teaching these subjects to children at an earlier age. Obviously the material here is simpler in nature than it would be were it to be addressed to teenagers or adults but I believe the foundational truth of the person of Christ can still be communicated (with relevance) to the pre-teen age group. This book will work by itself in communicating the person of Christ but I feel it would be most beneficial to follow it up with the Easter story and the work of Christ.

How to use these books

Each book is divided into five sections. Each section contains one lesson plan, three overhead sheets, one in-class worksheet and one take-home sheet, with the exception of the last section which includes two additional sheets (I hope that there will be more than enough material for each session – far better to have to leave some out than be left short and have to make some up!)

Lesson plan

Before arriving at the lesson, make sure you've read the complete lesson plan! It may seem obvious but making sure you understand and agree with the contents will help you as you lead the meeting.

Each lesson plan begins with a Bible Reading (or a Background Information section where necessary, to be read out first). All Readings and verses throughout these books are taken from the NIV Bible, unless otherwise stated. The verses that correspond to the overhead pictures are listed in order so that the picture can be placed up when the verse is reached.

The main teaching on the reading is in the form of questions to be read out to the children and 'desired answers'. Make sure you have read the desired answers and lesson summaries and then, bearing those answers in mind, gently lead the discussion and the children's responses introducing the given answers along the way. (The answers are written in such a way that they can be read out if discussion proves difficult at times.)

Helpful points

- It is most important to encourage the children to think about and understand the story and the questions themselves. Do not step in with the 'answers' too quickly!
- Make sure that the children address each section before moving on – further explanation or re-reading may be necessary.
- Try and involve *all* the children. This may mean addressing the questions to specific individuals, or asking the children if they agree with any opinions offered, etc.
- Above all be encouraging! Make sure they know when they're right but don't feel silly if they're wrong.
- The additional material is there to be used where appropriate or practical. Worksheets are explained where necessary and puzzles that require answers in the take-home sheet are given.
- Each session ends with a prayer that can either be prayed by you or by one of the children.

Overheads

There are three overhead illustrations for each section. (If appropriate these can also be photocopied on to plain paper and used as colouring sheets.)

Worksheets

These are intended to be completed in lesson time, but most will work equally well as take-home sheets if necessary.

Take-home sheets

When answers are needed they are given in the lesson plan. Since the take-home sheets often contain questions relevant to the reading, I suggest that the sheets are brought back completed the following week and the answers given in class. This should encourage the children to complete the readings and questions as well as the puzzles.

I hope that these books prove helpful to you – please write to Kevin Mayhew Publishers with comments, ideas or suggestions that might be included in further work.

EPISODE 1

Sin

EPISODE 1 — Sin

Reading

Matthew 26:20-29

Lesson objective

To recognise how hopeless the problem of sin in our lives would be if it were not for Jesus.

Background information

What we know as the 'Easter story' begins on Palm Sunday, the day when Jesus entered Jerusalem on a donkey. The crowd, imagining he had come to become their king and save them from their enemies, welcomed him with praising and cheering. However, it soon became obvious that Jesus wasn't going to be a king like they thought. Little did anybody know that rejecting and killing him was exactly what was needed to save them!

Overheads

1 (background information) Jesus enters Jerusalem
2 (v 25) Jesus speaks to Judas
3 (v 26) Jesus breaks the bread

Discussion questions and desired answers

Read verse 28 again. What does Jesus say his blood is for?
The forgiveness of sins.

In order to understand the forgiveness of sin we need to make sure we understand exactly what 'sin' is. What do you think sin is?
Sin is any action, thought, attitude or motive that goes against, or does not live up to, God's standards.

God is completely holy and perfect – what do you think his standards are?
They are 100 per cent perfect too. That means our every thought, word, action and motive must be 100 per cent pure and blameless – full of love and respect for God and other people – in order to reach those standards. Anything even slightly short fails!

Sometimes we might think that we don't sin very much or that we're really not too bad a person. Read Romans 3:23. What does this mean?
It means every person who has ever lived has sinned and therefore fallen short of God's standards! Everyone has sinned and therefore has sin in them.

If everybody has sin in them where does that leave us with God?
Separated from him! God is perfect and sin is not. God cannot have anything to do with sin because the imperfection that is sin cannot possibly be joined to the perfection that is God! (Use a visual illustration here of two magnets – turn them so that they naturally repel each other. This is like God and sin – they simply cannot be joined.

It would be impossible for the perfection of God to take into itself the imperfection of sin. Sin is repelled. We are separated.)

Not only are we separated from God by our sin but we should also be punished for failing to meet his perfect standards. Read Romans 6:23. What is the punishment for sin?

Death!

So are we right in saying that every person who has ever lived is a sinner, separated from God, and that their sin will end in death?

Yes we are! (Now ask the children, 'Should we end the lesson there then, since that seems pretty final? . . . why not?' Hopefully somebody will mention Jesus. Read Matthew 26:28 again if necessary.)

Jesus said his blood would forgive sins, so thankfully this isn't the end of the story. There is a way back to God that we will look at in the coming weeks. But remember – if it wasn't for Jesus the story really would end there – with no escaping the fact that we are sinners facing death!

Additional material

Fun

'Donkey racing' Group Game. While Jesus didn't exactly gallop into Jerusalem, he did ride on a donkey – and therein lies the connection! In pairs or teams have time trials over a set distance with the 'donkey' on all fours and the rider on their back. Alternatively, Jesus rode over the crowd's garments and cloaks. In two teams see which donkey and rider can ride over the most jumpers, coats and so on, the fastest over a set distance. These could be picked up by other team members once the rider has passed over them and quickly moved to the front again. Some light-hearted relief after being told we're all sinners destined to die!

Worksheet

Let the children attempt the maze and see if they can answer the question – the correct answer eventually being 'none of them'! We run into sin in everything we do because sin is actually *in us*. *We* are the problem and *we* need to be changed on the inside! That is why the solution only works from the other side – only God can actually do something about sin. Start from God on the maze and you'll soon find your way back to us!

Take-home sheet

Clockwise from Jesus: 10 John, 1 James, 6 Philip, 11 Bartholomew, 4 James, 5 Simon, 3 Thaddaeus, 12 Judas, 2 Thomas, 8 Matthew, 9 Andrew and 7 Peter.

Closing prayer

Dear Father God, I recognise that I am a sinner and that I can never change the fact that I have never and will never reach your perfect standards. I am unworthy of knowing you and yet I know that you love me so much you have made it possible, through Jesus, for me to be your closest friend. Father, I look forward to learning more about what Jesus has done for me. Please help me to understand. Amen.

In today's episode we learnt that sin is a barrier which separates us from God.
Which of these things below that we can do will overcome that barrier and unite us with God?
The black fuzz represents sin – if you run into sin then you need to go back to another option . . .

THE LAST SUPPER

Before the events of the crucifixion Jesus shared a final meal with his disciples. Once you have solved the anagrams at the foot of the page, cut out the disciples and arrange them around the table using the clues to position them correctly!

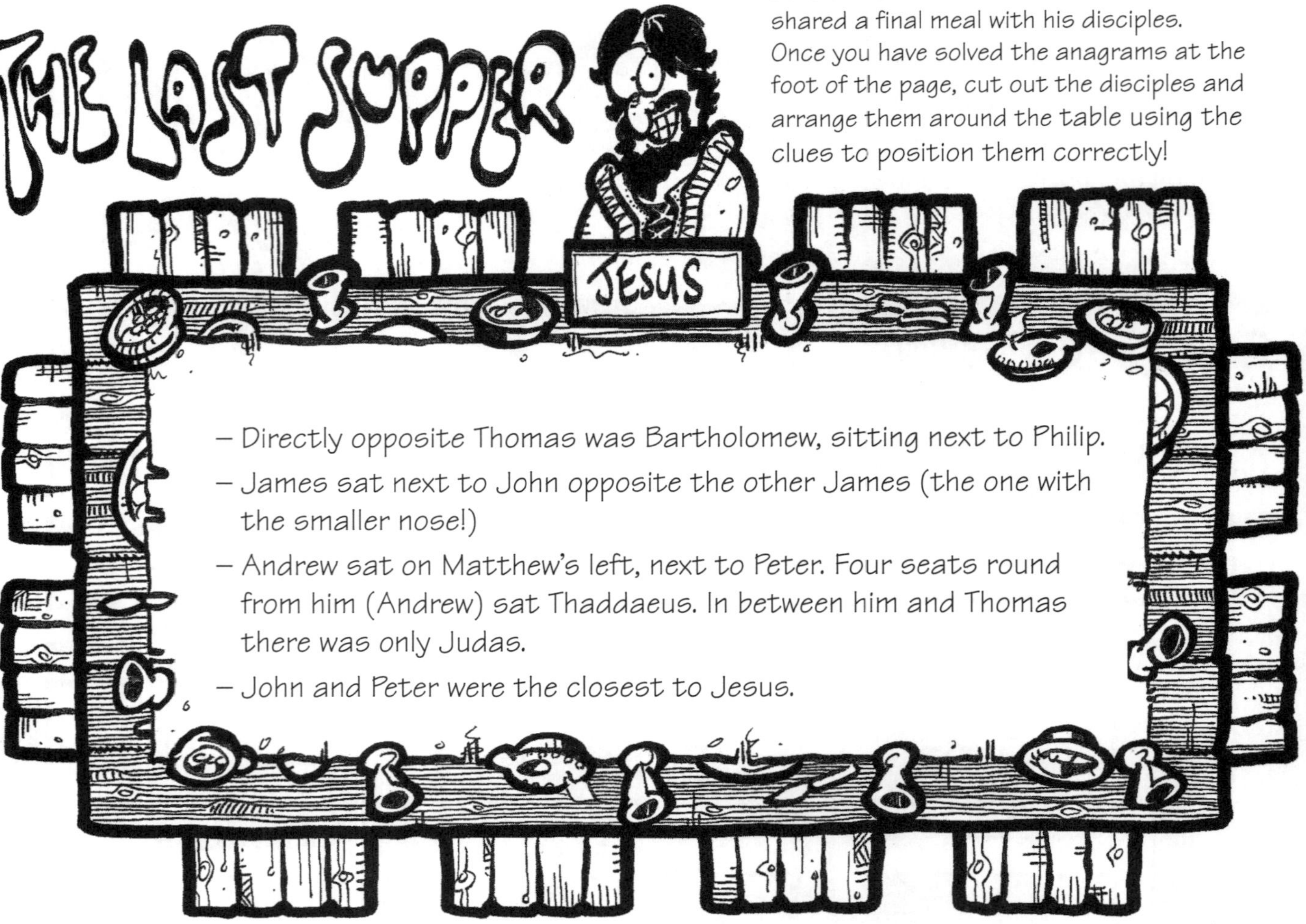

– Directly opposite Thomas was Bartholomew, sitting next to Philip.

– James sat next to John opposite the other James (the one with the smaller nose!)

– Andrew sat on Matthew's left, next to Peter. Four seats round from him (Andrew) sat Thaddaeus. In between him and Thomas there was only Judas.

– John and Peter were the closest to Jesus.

Using Matthew 10:2-4 unscramble the names of the 12 disciples below and write them into the appropriate boxes.....

1. SEMJA 2. ATHSMO 3. EDADSATHU 4. MEJAS 5. NISMO
6. HILPIP 7. ETREP 8. THATWEM 9. WEDRAN 10. NOJH
11. MOOLWABTRE 12. JUDJA

EPISODE 2

The Substitute

EPISODE 2

The Substitute

Reading

Luke 22:39-46; Matthew 26:47-56

Lesson objective

To communicate the idea of substitution – Jesus died in our place.

Overheads

1 (Luke 22:42) Jesus prays
2 (Matthew 26:50) Jesus speaks to Judas
3 (Matthew 26:52) Jesus calls out to stop the violence

Discussion questions and desired answers

Jesus was very frightened as he prayed. What do you think scared him the most?

(The children will no doubt refer to the physical pain of the cross.)

True – the pain would be terrible – but something even worse was involved! In order to understand we need to first realise what was actually going to happen on the cross. Last episode we learnt that everybody is a sinner and that their sin not only separates them from God but deserves to be punished. What was the punishment for sin?

Death.

In the Old Testament God set up a system involving death that enabled people to be forgiven for their sins. Do you know what that was?

Animal sacrifices. When a person sinned they should really have died, but instead they sacrificed a perfect animal and apologised to God. God looked upon the blood of the animal (blood represents life) like it was the blood of the person, i.e. that they had died and the necessary punishment had been met.

The animal that was sacrificed was a 'substitute'. Do you know what that means here?

It means that the animal died *instead* of the sinner. The punishment due to the sinner was still paid for but by the blood of the animal sacrifice in the sinner's place. That way the sinner didn't have to actually die and could still be in relationship with God.

Read John 1:29. What does John say about Jesus?

Jesus is 'the Lamb of God who takes away the sin of the world'.

The animals that were sacrificed had to be completely perfect and healthy. We know that Jesus lived a completely perfect life. How do you think this is relevant to what John said about him?

John calls Jesus a 'lamb' and since we know that Jesus was perfect we can see that John is saying Jesus is exactly like a perfect animal sacrifice. However, John says that Jesus is not just a sacrifice for one person, but a sacrifice for the entire world – for everyone!

So if the blood of a perfect animal sacrifice acted as a substitute for the blood of a sinner, what was Jesus – whom John called a lamb (perfect animal sacrifice) to take away the sin of the world – going to do on the cross?

Jesus substituted his own life as a sacrifice for us. Just as the animal sacrifices previously bore the punishment for the sinner's sin (death) instead of the sinner, so Jesus bore the punishment for the entire world – for you and me – instead of us having to. That is why we say Jesus died for our sins.

Although Jesus had never sinned, he took on himself the punishment due to sinners because, as Peter says, 'He bore our sins in his body' (1 Peter 2:24). So Jesus took our sins into himself on the cross and was punished for them, instead of us. Can you remember what sin does to our relationship with God?

It separates us.

So what happened to Jesus when he took our sins into his body on the cross?

He was separated from God. ('My God! Why have you abandoned me?' Mark 15:34)

This was the thing that we spoke of earlier that scared Jesus the most. Somehow, although Jesus and the Father are one, when Jesus took sin into himself for us, they were torn apart. Whenever we think of the physical pain of the cross we should remember that we can't even begin to understand that separation. Jesus faced that separation from God for us. He did it for all of us in our place – a substitute. Next episode we will look at how that affects us.

Additional material

Fun

'Sleeping Disciples' Group Game. All the children are to be disciples and lie on the floor with their eyes closed. You as the teacher (or someone else) are to be Jesus. Ensure there are the same amount of chairs as 'disciples' scattered about the room, then when you are ready ask, 'Who's sleeping?' The disciples must all leap up shouting 'Not me!' and sit on an available chair. Repeat this but whilst the disciples are 'sleeping', move the chairs around and and remove one, like musical chairs. Gradually the children will be 'out' as they fail to get to a chair in time, until only one is left: the winner!

Worksheet

Self-explanatory. (You will need scissors and tape or glue.)

Take-home sheet

The verse is 'Look, the Lamb of God who takes away the sins of the world.'

The squares not in the picture are C, D and F.

Closing prayer

Dear Lord Jesus, when I think of the pain and the separation from God that you experienced on the cross, I feel so undeserving – that you would go through all that just for me. Thank you, Jesus, that I am so valuable to you. Please help me to realise more fully the price you paid and what it means to me. I love you, Lord. Amen.

Fill in your name in the boxes on the cross below.
That sounds pretty bleak doesn't it – and without Jesus there would be nothing left to say.
Cut out the shapes opposite and stick them over the cross. When you've finished look up 1 Peter 2:24 and write it on to the finished cross, substituting your name where the verse says 'our'.

The Substitute

WHICH OF THE SQUARES ARE NOT PART OF THE BIG PICTURE BELOW?

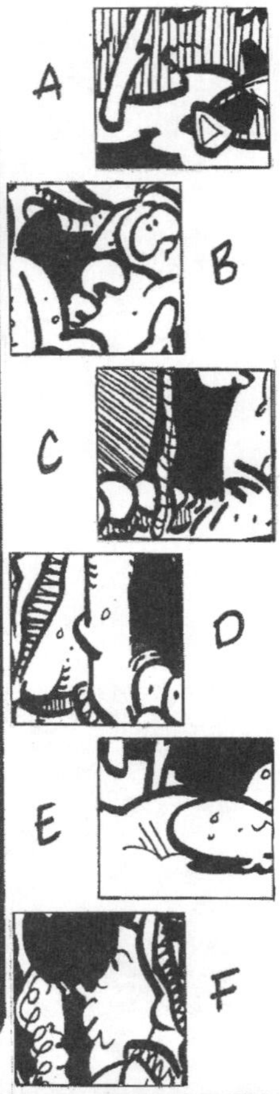

Work out below the words John the Baptist said when he saw Jesus

Do not read the questions yet! Study the picture of John greeting Jesus on the banks of the River Jordan for two minutes then cover it up and try and answer the following questions. (Maybe a friend could read the questions out.)

- Were there any birds in the picture?
- What was Jesus holding?
- How many people were there?
- What did John have on his feet?
- How many animals were there?
- Was the man with the stick holding it in his right or left hand?
- How many bulrushes were there?
- How many pairs of eyes were there in the picture?

EPISODE 3

God's Gift to Us

EPISODE 3 God's Gift to Us

Reading

Mark 15:1-15

Lesson objective

To understand the exchange that takes place when we accept that Jesus died for our sins – our sin is passed to him – his righteousness is credited to us.

Background information

Jesus was taken before the Jewish priests and elders where all kinds of accusations were made against him. They had no evidence of any wrong he had done but feared that people were following him and turning away from their strict religious system, so they made charges against Jesus and found him guilty. In order to sentence him to death the official Roman trial would have to find Jesus guilty too, so the priests took him to Pilate, the Roman governor.

Overheads

1 (Background information) The High Priest accuses Jesus
2 (v 4) Pilate accuses Jesus
3 (v 13) The crowd condemns Jesus

Discussion questions and desired answers

During his trial Jesus had the opportunity to defend himself, maybe even get himself released. Read verse 5 again. What did he say and why?
Nothing. Jesus had to die – it was what he had come to do and he intended to go through with it.

Jesus had to die because sin had to be dealt with. What did we learn about Jesus' death last week?
That it was a substitute for our own death – he took our sin and the punishment we really deserved and died for it in our place.

So is everybody now forgiven? Do we have to do anything for it?
Everybody is forgiven when they believe what Jesus did for them and accept it as true in their own lives.

This is called faith. Faith is believing something is true. With faith we believe Jesus died in our place taking our deserved punishment. What then happens to our sin from God's point of view?
It is put on Jesus and the price is paid. We are left without sin only because of Jesus.

The Bible calls this 'justification'. Through faith we accept Jesus' work and God justifies us, making us right in his sight. God gives us something amazing! Read Romans 4:23-24. What does God give ('credit') to us?
Righteousness.

What does righteousness mean?

It is perfect holiness – a pure, spotless, perfect spirit free from sin!

Read 1 Corinthians 1:30. Where does this righteousness come from?

Jesus! It is Jesus' perfect life!

When we believe and accept (through faith) that Jesus died for us, an exchange – a swap takes place. Can you see what it is?

We give our sinful life to Jesus (who has already paid the price for it) and God freely gives us Jesus' righteousness!

Isn't that amazing! Suddenly in God's sight we are born again! Instead of having sin we begin a brand-new life with Jesus' righteousness. It is God's gift to us and known as 'grace' – something we don't deserve but which God freely gives us! We might ask, however, isn't our new life, our righteousness, spoilt when we next sin? Read John 13:6-11. What does Jesus say here and what did he mean?

If you've had a bath you're clean. From then on only the soles of your feet get dirty as you walk about. Jesus is saying that once God has declared you righteous (made you clean) nothing can change that! Any future sin is just like a bit of dirt on your feet – ask Jesus to forgive it and it's gone. But righteousness doesn't go, it's yours. It may seem too good to be true but that's what makes grace so amazing! God loves us so much he has made a flawless way to get rid of sin through Jesus! Next episode we'll see how Jesus' righteousness in us can give us true relationship with God.

Additional material

Visual aid

Find a jar with a screw-on lid and make it dirty inside and out. Tell the children this represents their lives. Only God is able to get the lid off. In accepting Jesus, God cleanses us completely. Christ's righteousness is sealed inside us (wash the jar completely clean and screw the lid on tight – sealed for good). Future sin is like dirt that can be wiped off the outside of the glass (illustrate this) – once God has declared you righteous nothing changes that. The amazing thing about grace is that even if we let the outside of the jar get dirty the inside remains clean! That cleanness – Christ's righteousness is ours by faith and grace and will stay ours!

Worksheet

1 mud, 2 sin, 3 ourselves, 4 bath, 5 wash, 6 death, 7 Jesus, 8 clean, 9 faith, 10 never, 11 dirt, 12 soles, 13 feet, 14 disciples, 15 apologise, 16 forgive.

Take-home sheet

Line 3 is 'righteousness' (1 rhinoceros, 2 refrigerator, 4 restaurant)

Closing prayer

Dear Father God, your goodness to me is just amazing! It is incredible that you see in me the righteousness of your Son, Jesus, when I accept him. Thank you for taking my old sinful life away for ever. You are such a good God and I want to live my life in a way that shows how thankful I am. Please help me, Lord Jesus. Amen.

At the foot of the page are 16 words. Can you put the appropriate words into the correct spaces to complete the text below? (Based on the story of Jesus washing our feet in John 13:3-10.) When you've finished, try finding all 16 words in the wordsearch!

As people we are all covered in 1. ______ 1. ______ represents 2. ______ and no matter how hard we try we just can't get rid of it by 3. ______

Just like taking a 4. ______ 5. ______es away 1. ______, so the 6. ______ of 7. ______ has the power to 5. ______ away all of our 2. ______

Once we have had a 4. ______ we are completely 8. ______ When we accept 7. ______ through 9. ______ God says that we become 8. ______ inside. All of our 2. ______ is gone!

Once 7. ______ 5. ______es us 8. ______ we will 10. ______ be covered in 1. ______ (that is 2. ______) again! From then on all 2. ______s are no more than 11. ______ on the 12. ______ of our 13. ______.

Just as 7. ______ 5. ______ed his 14. ______ 13. ______ so he will 5. ______ ours. That means that when we 2. ______ we 15. ______ to 7. ______ and he will 16. ______ us, just like 5. ______ing the 11. ______ from our 13. ______

v n e y b d d c q a i x c u s a r q h j f x r c q p
i q i s p a o i f c b y p a k s j y d s b c f t p g c w e w t x y s
s j t z a x a r e z e j l e i a b s w t g a p n t f d c k b d l j
a p d r u p n h h t i a f v t z x q e r x e o r y b v l h u s u z p
i h j q w v c j s g r h l b j h r z l e d y d o q g e i q a v m k i
t r k a o b q f q t s e o m v a k s o i i v e s u a t r y l r l m t
b k s v f j w g o u s t k c g g t p s f r e v e n h e f m b j c s h
o j b w y r m k n r h v q n s b o c g u t z n m v s i p e n k r n q
h e g l k c f h u v g f l i p e i u n j i h u x t a d j o e f m o u
n s x g s a p o l o g i s e f p l n i n s j g l y m b n z o t x d g
c u d m x i u f w l i u v d l c w v o a h c y w x b a z u c g p n v
y s c z d t g l o x m w m e q f m k w q k m k h l b a t h w h e q p
e f n l l e n d p z j g s n e d p l m l v i b z z c k q a p d o f w
u m z m e n k o p x n o r e a f d j w r s t v l e x a

bath
feet
forgive
clean
ourselves
death
soles
disciples
mud
wash
jesus
sin
apologise
faith
never
dirt

... Jesus on Trial ...

The same crowd that praised Jesus on Palm Sunday now shout for his crucifixion.
Below are two crowd pictures. In the second everyone has moved around, two new people appear and three disappear. Can you circle the missing ones in the first picture and the new ones in the second?

What do we get as a gift from God when we believe in Jesus?
Below are four answers split into syllables. Can you uncover one answer per line and determine which line holds the correct answer?

EPISODE 4

Reconciliation

EPISODE 4 Reconciliation

Reading

Matthew 27:38-51, 54

Lesson objective

To communicate how the death of Jesus has opened the way for relationship with God.

Background information

The soldiers beat Jesus and twisted a crown of thorns onto his head before forcing him to carry his cross through the crowded streets. At Golgotha he was tied and nailed to the wooden cross with a sign above his head that read 'This is Jesus – the King of the Jews'.

Overheads

1 (background information) Jesus carries his cross
2 (v 41) Jesus on the cross
3 (v 16) Jesus cries his last words

Discussion questions and desired answers

Read John 19:30. What are Jesus' last words?
'It is finished.'

What is finished? (Read John 4:34 for a clue if necessary)
The work the Father (God) gave him to do.

Jesus' work was to deal with the problem of sin in our lives. Can you remember what sin does to our relationship with God?
It separates us.

So why did Jesus deal with sin?
So that we wouldn't be separated from God.

This is also known as 'reconciliation'. To reconcile means to make relationship where there was a problem. In this case sin was the problem that stopped us being able to have a relationship with God. Jesus has dealt with that problem and by accepting him we can be reconciled with God. An example of this truth is in today's reading. What happened in verse 51?
The curtain of the temple was torn in two when Jesus died.

The curtain in the Temple was the entrance to the 'Holy of Holies' – the most sacred chamber where the presence of God dwelt! Only one person could come into God's presence through the curtain – the High Priest, and only once a year. Why do you think the curtain tore when Jesus died?
To show us that the way to God is now open to us too.

The Bible calls Jesus 'the High Priest' and in Ephesians 3:17 Paul says that as Christians we have the Spirit of Jesus in our hearts. With Jesus inside us we can therefore go into God's presence. What do we mean by saying we are free to go into his presence or that we can 'come to God'?

We mean that there are no longer any rituals or animal sacrifices that make us right with God. Jesus inside us is what makes us right. He has been the sacrifice, he has paid the price and he now lives in our hearts. Coming to God because of this means that we can have a personal relationship with God – we can talk to him, pray and sing to him, feel his love and his presence, have him talk to us and answer our prayers, all because of Jesus.

Sometimes we feel like we can't be good enough to have a relationship with God or that it's something only for other people and not us. Sometimes we feel too bad or too unlovable to be accepted. Is any of this ever true?

No, never! When we become a Christian we have the spirit of Jesus and his gift of righteousness in our hearts. No one who is a Christian has more or less of Jesus and his gift than anyone else! We can be sure that we are accepted by God because we know with 100 per cent certainty that God accepts his Son Jesus, and if we have Jesus inside us then obviously we are accepted too!

Can you see how amazing Jesus' death was, and how necessary! We are free from the sin in our hearts which separates us from God because we have Jesus and his righteousness in our hearts instead! We are free to be joined in relationship with God. Next episode we'll see the final reasons why we can be sure all these things are true!

Additional material

Fun

Ask the children to imagine that God is behind a particular door in the room. Ask for a volunteer to go through and see God. First, they are required to solve the answers to five ridiculously hard maths questions (square roots of large numbers, etc.). This represents the standards we have to meet to enter God's presence. It's impossible for us. Jesus' death not only opened the door to God (symbolised by the torn curtain) but then gives us a fulfilling life. This is represented by the teacher having the answers to the questions worked out and written onto rice paper for the volunteer to eat. Jesus has done everything that was needed and then lives in us. All we have to do is believe and accept him then we have all we need to enter God's presence. Emphasise that it is *only* through Jesus that we can come before God.

Worksheet

This is the cover to a personal diary for the children to record their relationship with God. This can be very encouraging to look back on later. There is space on the cover for them to personalise it.

Take-home sheet

Crown of thorns number one. Code 'draw near to God'.

Closing prayer

Dear Lord Jesus, thank you that you have come to live in my heart and make it possible for me to have a relationship with God the Father. Lord Jesus, I know that I am accepted by God because you're there with me and that wherever else I go and whatever else I do you are always with me. Thank you, Jesus. Amen.

Jesus died to take away the problem of sin which separated me from God. Now, having dealt with the problem once and for all, Jesus lives in my heart and I am free to have a relationship with God who loves me.

This is a personal diary of my relationship with God, the things he's taught and told me, the prayers he's heard and answered, how I've felt about him (good or bad!), what he's done for me, what I've done for him. Basically, anything at all to do with me and God – the friendship we have because of Jesus.

On the cross

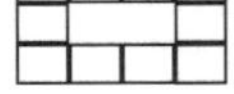

Below is a picture of Jesus on the cross, surrounded by Roman soldiers and his followers. Can you separate the soldiers and followers . . .

Join all the dots together using ruler-straight lines so that all the soldiers are on one side and the followers on the other.

Which silhouette below matches the crown of thorns?

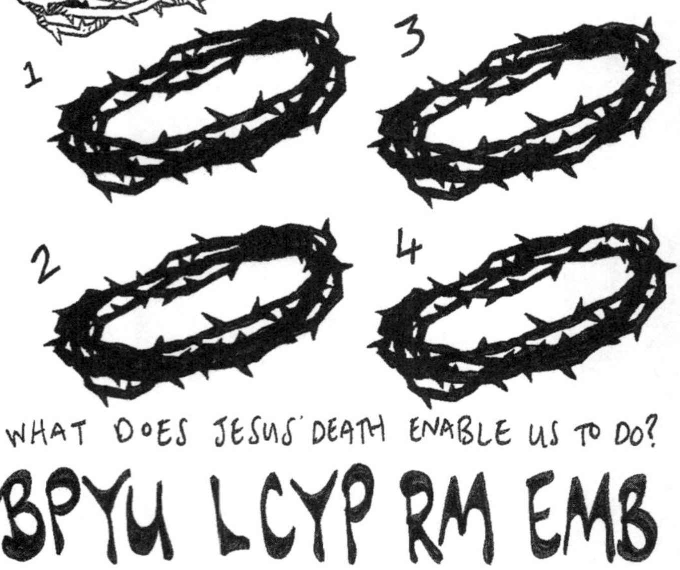

WHAT DOES JESUS' DEATH ENABLE US TO DO?

BPYU LCYP RM EMB

_ _ _ _   _ _ _ _   _ _   _ _ _

FTCY PGCT VQ IQF

CRACK THE CODE TO REVEAL THE ANSWER...

... CLUE (if you want it!): IN THE MIDDLE!

Can you cut out these squares below and make a picture of the crown of thorns out of them? The shape of the final picture is shown above.

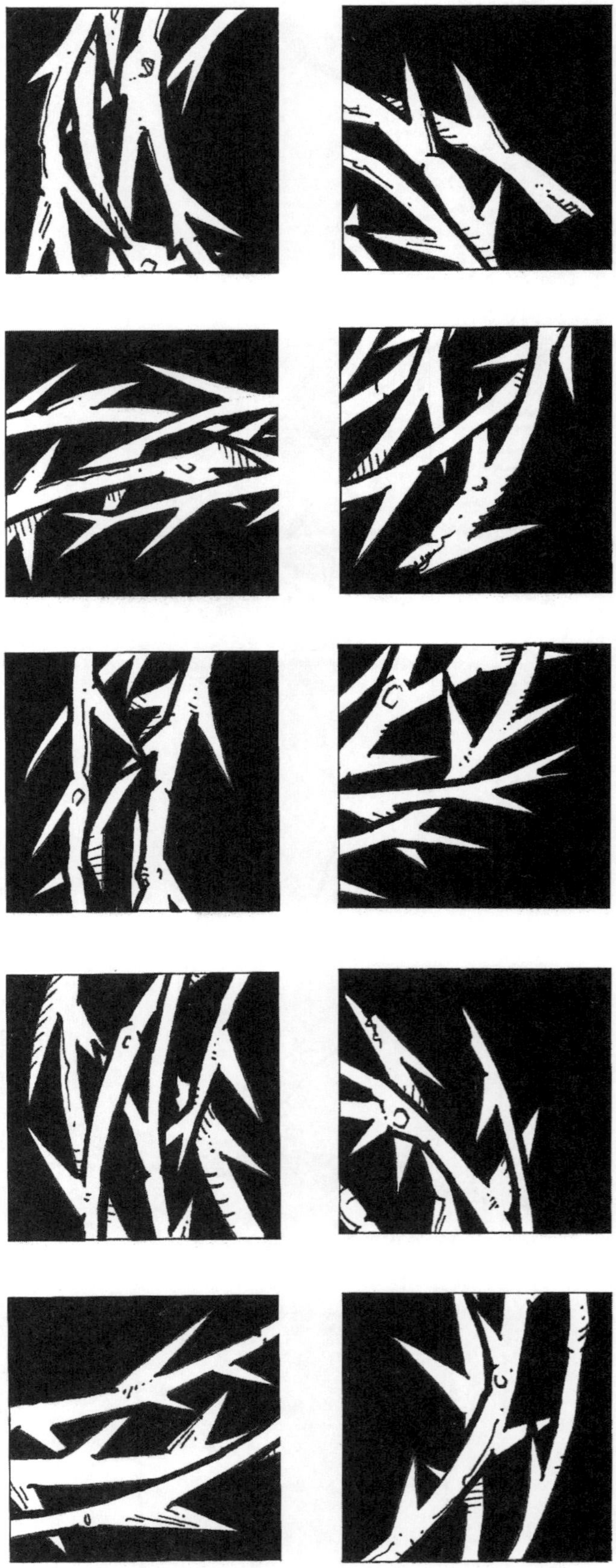

EPISODE 5

Children of God

EPISODE 5

Children of God

Reading

John 20:1-18

Lesson objective

To communicate the security of being an adopted child of God and co-heir with Christ.

Background information

When Jesus had died some of his followers asked for permission to take his body and lay it in a tomb in a special garden. Pilate agreed and the tomb was sealed with a large stone.

Overheads

1 (v 1) Mary visits the tomb
2 (v 4) Two disciples reach the empty tomb
3 (v 16) Jesus appears to Mary

Discussion questions and desired answers

We have seen that Jesus paid the price of sin for each and every one of us. Through faith in Jesus we can be forgiven and have a relationship with God. What happened in today's reading and who is stronger, Jesus or death?

Jesus rose from the dead. He came back to life and has beaten death. He is stronger than death.

This is how we can be certain that Jesus' death is effective in forgiving our sins. He bore sin's punishment then rose again. Sin's punishment is over, it is in the past. Now the punishment isn't the end after all – Jesus' resurrection life is now inside us. And that's not all. Read Romans 8:15-17. What does Paul call us as Christians here?

Children of God and co-heirs with Christ.

When you become a Christian and Jesus comes to live in you, you are 'adopted' into God's family and become a 'child of God'. Paul also said we are heirs with Christ. Do you know what an heir is and what being co-heirs with Christ means?

It is somebody who is legally or officially entitled to inherit something, e.g. the son of a rich father would be heir to his father's wealth. Becoming children of God makes us as much a child of God as Jesus himself is, all that belongs to him belongs to us too!

Read Luke 24:51. What happens to Jesus and what does this mean for us?

Jesus ascends back into heaven to be with God for ever. This is eaxctly the same for us, we will be with Jesus eternally in heaven!

Does that mean we will not physically die?

No, all of us will die at some point but as we know, Jesus has beaten death and it is no longer the end. We will go to be with God to receive our inheritance.

Does going to heaven depend on how good we are and how well we live?

No, just like our righteousness it depends on Jesus, not on us. God will always see our spirits as righteous (pure and holy) because it is Jesus' righteousness in us, given as a gift, and we know that Jesus' righteousness can't change. In the same way, we have been adopted by God, declared to be one of his children. Just as we know God will never forsake his Son, Jesus, so he will never forsake his adopted children – us. We can be 100 per cent certain that when we die we will go to heaven.

Isn't that amazing! God really does love us that much and now we can see that knowing God, being in relationship with him and knowing that we will one day be with him are possible only because of Jesus and our inviting him into our hearts.

Additional material

Prayer

Take time to check that all the children who want to have invited Jesus into their hearts. Some might simply have been coming to church and never asked him for themselves.

Fun

'In their midst!' Group Game. Based loosely on the idea of Jesus appearing in the midst of the disciples after he'd risen. Designate an area in the centre of the room to be 'the midst'. The idea is for one person to end up there without being caught. All the children bar one are disciples and must wander round the room but keep out of that area. On the command 'stop' they freeze and close their eyes. The child who was selected must then attempt to navigate through the frozen disciples and appear undetected 'in their midst'. If a disciple senses them brushing past they may make an attempt to grab them, still with their eyes shut. If successful that person is out and the game starts again. If unsuccessful, however, that disciple is out and the ungrabbed child may proceed.

Pick a scene

Have the children either draw or write about their favourite aspect or scene covered in the five episodes. Work could be displayed in the church or some form of drama could be presented.

Summary sheet

The teaching of all five episodes summarised for the children to take home and refer to in the future.

Worksheet

Self-explanatory.

Take-home sheet

Square A5

Closing prayer

Dear Father God, how can I ever thank you enough for all you have done for me? Thank you, Father, for Jesus and that you have adopted me as if I were your very own child and that one day I will be with you for ever. You are so good to me and I am so privileged to be able to truly call you my heavenly Father – my dad. I love you, Father God. Amen.

Summary sheet

God is perfect. We as people are not, because of sin.[1] The imperfection of sin cannot come anywhere near the perfection of God and so we are consequently separated from God by sin.

The punishment for sin is death.[2] In the past people sacrificed perfect animals and God overlooked their sin by treating the animal's blood as if it were their own. The animal was a substitute for the sinner – it died in their place.[3]

Jesus lived a perfect life and substituted himself as our sacrifice.[4] He died for all the sins we would commit[5] so that we wouldn't have to and so that we could be forgiven.[6]

Through faith we can choose to believe and accept this.[7] When this happens we pass our sin to Jesus (who has already paid the price) and he gives us perfect life – his righteousness – in our hearts.[8] His righteousness is an unchanging gift to us.[9] We are justified before God not through anything we've done but through Jesus' life inside us.[10]

Instead of being separated from God we can now be reconciled to him and have relationship.[11] When we come to God he doesn't see our sin but rather the perfect life of his Son Jesus in us. We are adopted as God's own children[12] and declared to be joint heirs with Jesus.[13]

The resurrection life of Jesus in us[14] assures us that physical death is no longer the end and we can look forward to receiving our inheritance – eternal life and relationship with our heavenly Father.[15]

All of this is only possible through accepting and receiving Jesus.[16]

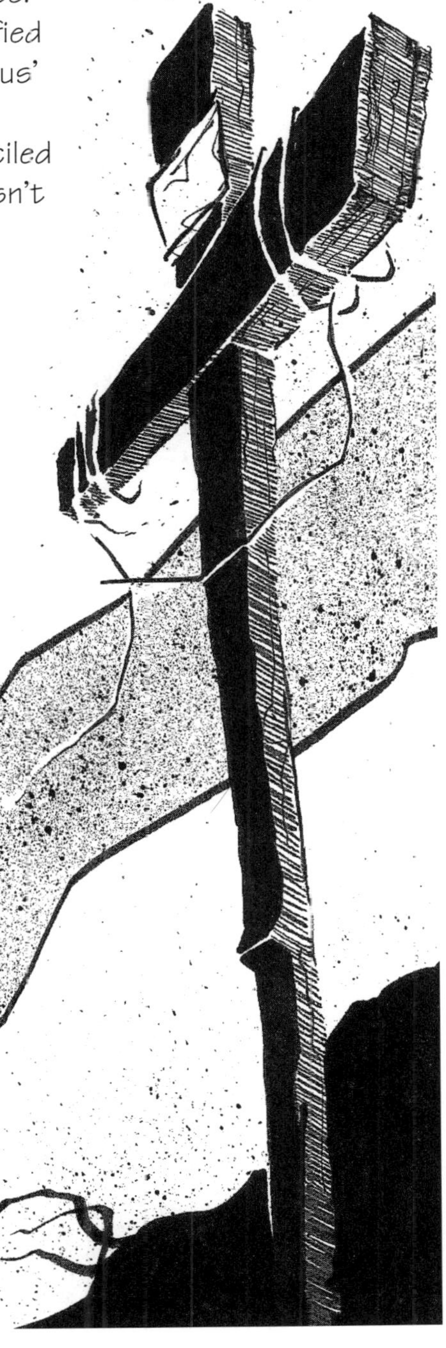

[1] Romans 3:23
[2] Romans 6:23
[3] Hebrews 9:13, 22
[4] 1 John 1:21
[5] Isaiah 53: 5-6
[6] Colossians 1:14
[7] Acts 10:43
[8] Philippians 3:9
[9] Hebrews 10:10
[10] Romans 5:1
[11] Romans 5:11
[12] John 1:12-13
[13] Romans 8:15-17
[14] Colossians 1:27
[15] 1 Peter 1:3-4
[16] John 14:6

Read Galatians 4:6-7 (NIV translation). Paul is talking about our new relationship with God through Jesus. Can you find the verses in a continual line in the grid? The verse may go forwards, backwards, up or down but not diagonally.

```
p x a s z y p d f r e s o r a s
w r b s n o s e r a g w n k c z
j c o g s b r s q u y l q x p t
a q d h g c n o e o h v m b u d
k c i t o m j n i y z n d j y e
h d m l d g s s k e s u a c e b
e l g u n k o g x n a e f j o i r u w l z s o n
b f n d o c a o m l f g c i l p i x e r s i t i
i d f v n j t d s e n t t h e s b m v n g h k n
a c o h w c y s o v p b h k s p i r i t o f a t
l e o b t z a e n t t g h m p c p i f q f j d o
l e f i i u w r s e n t i r i a d o h c h b f e
s o u v r x s q u t g h n i m o u t p v i s s d
o g t n i p s e h t s t r a e h r u o s y q o z
u g a f b x j w y o u a r e k g o t n i n e
t d b b a f a k o n j l o n l c u r a i q
h a b e l i t o s d y o u n g k w b x n t
o s a p c g h e r s o n a j c m l r o
n q t m z n v y a r e g f o
a t u b e v a l s u e s u
n e a f d u a e t f j a t r
d r b e a s o n g o d n b s a
s b s r t l d k b r h s z r
i a c a y e d a m g a w c
n r c u o r i e o v s h j
c e y o u a n h s l a i x
```

What does the very last word of the verse mean?

____

How is that relevant to you?

____

____

____

He's alive!

After Jesus rose again he appeared to his disciples and friends often before finally going back to heaven. On one occasion he joined two men as they walked on the road to a place called Emmaus. From one of the men's brief recollections below can you work out whereabouts on the map that Jesus joined them?
(Read the story in Luke 24:13-32 if you like.)

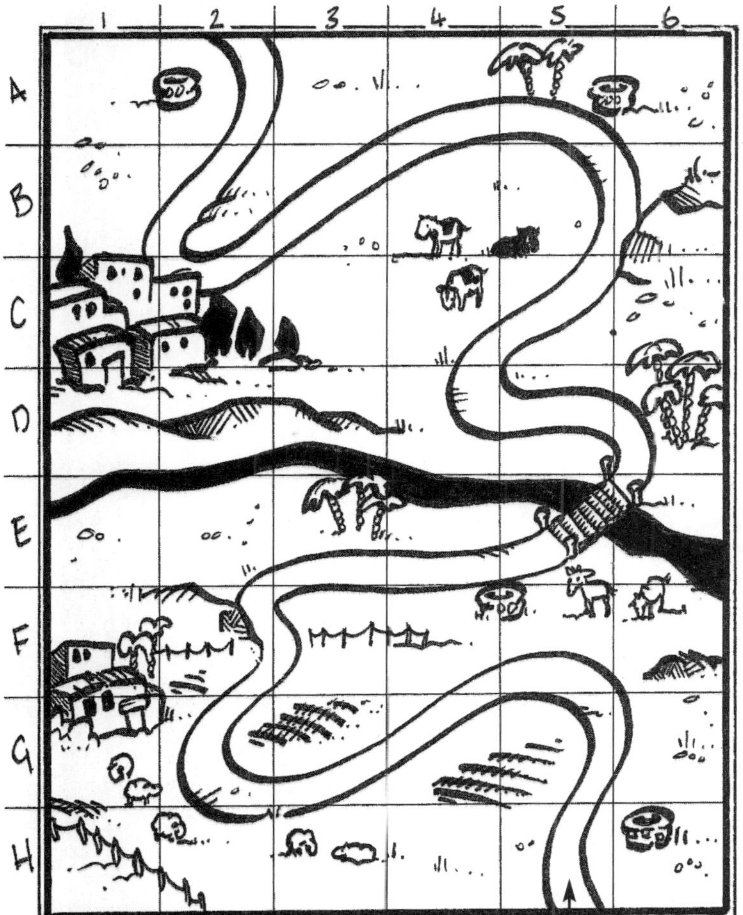

(use the travellers' left and right - not yours looking on)

It was very hot that day and I remember that we stopped straight away at the first well on our right. Travelling on we passed some houses. We stopped again at the next well for more water. After the well we passed some animals on the right before crossing the bridge. We travelled on past some trees and more animals and had just stopped at the well on the right when a stranger joined us. Of course, we didn't know who it was then . . .

Can you spot the 10 differences below?